A LifeGuide®

INTEGRITY
Living the Truth

**10 studies
for individuals or groups**

Carolyn Nystrom

With Notes for Leaders

InterVarsity Press
Downers Grove, Illinois

InterVarsity Press
P.O. Box 1400, Downers Grove, IL 60515
World Wide Web: www.ivpress.com
E-mail: mail@ivpress.com

Cover photograph: Dennis Flaherty

ISBN 0-8308-3052-9

Printed in the United States of America ∞

17	16	15	14	13	12	11	10	9	8	7	6	5	4	3
13	12	11	10	09	08	07	06	05	04	03	02	01		

Contents

GETTING THE MOST OUT OF *INTEGRITY* ———————— 4

1 **Imitate Jesus**   Mark 10:32-45 ————— 8

2 **Keep Commitments**   Hosea 1:1—2:1; 3 ————— 12

3 **Cultivate Endurance** Job 1:1—2:10 ————— 15

4 **Speak Truth**   Genesis 20 ————— 18

5 **Practice Self-Control** Judges 16 ————— 21

6 **Respect Your Body**   1 Corinthians 6:12-20—— 25

7 **Expect Temptation**   Genesis 39 ————— 29

8 **Guard Your Tongue**   James 3:1-12 ————— 33

9 **Offer Forgiveness**   John 21———— 37

10 **Trust God**   Psalm 25 ————— 41

Leader's Notes ————————————————— 44

Getting the Most Out of *Integrity*

Some words are rarely spoken in polite company. We hear them and cringe. But those words are changing. Some startling examples now appear on that "unspoken" list. How often, for example, do we hear the words *right* or *wrong* spoken by ordinary people? And when we hear these words, we see embarrassed shrugs—almost as an apology for using such bold words. Sure enough, a peacemaker is almost certain to introduce softer words as the conversation continues, words like *appropriate* and *inappropriate behavior,* as an inoffensive substitute for words that assume a moral standard regardless of personal convenience. Then everyone relaxes, relieved that no one really expects a universal standard.

Integrity assumes right and wrong. Sure, we don't have to announce this in a living room full of relativists. Integrity is quiet. It deals with the inside, with motives, with ideals, quiet things like keeping commitments—even the hard ones, as the prophet Hosea shows us. Integrity tells the truth—even if that truth might prove fatal, a test Abraham failed. Integrity expects temptation and braces for it—as did Joseph in the presence of the demanding wife of his employer. Integrity cultivates endurance—as did Job in the face of overwhelming tragedy. Integrity guards the tongue, channeling its power to encourage others and to glorify God. Integrity follows the path of forgiveness, a lesson Peter learned at the loving hand of his Lord. Integrity trusts God because in the end God alone is trustworthy. God's integrity is flawless.

Why live a life of integrity? Does integrity promise success? No, sometimes integrity will bring job loss and financial ruin. Does integrity bring respect from others? Perhaps, but likely only from those who also pursue this quiet goal. Does integrity mold healthy relationships? Integrity points us in that direction—but without guarantee. We see no evidence that Gomar ever willingly lived as Hosea's wife again. Does integrity make us happy? Maybe, but Job could never be considered happy as he sat sick and grieving in his pile of ashes with accusing friends at his side.

But integrity has its own reward. It allows us to pursue what is right and to reject what is wrong—even if we must whisper those words in a crowd. Integrity invites us to know ourselves and to grow in respect for what we see there. Integrity brings contentment. Integrity draws us to follow Christ as our model—and our Lord.

May these studies guide us toward integrity.

Suggestions for Individual Study

1. As you begin each study, pray that God will speak to you through his Word.

2. Read the introduction to the study and respond to the personal reflection question or exercise. This is designed to help you focus on God and on the theme of the study.

3. Each study deals with a particular passage—so that you can delve into the author's meaning in that context. Read and reread the passage to be studied. If you are studying a book, it will be helpful to read through the entire book prior to the first study. The questions are written using the language of the New International Version, so you may wish to use that version of the Bible. The New Revised Standard Version is also recommended.

4. This is an inductive Bible study, designed to help you discover for yourself what Scripture is saying. The study includes three types of questions. *Observation* questions ask about the basic facts: who, what, when, where and how. *Interpretation* questions delve into the meaning of the passage. *Application* questions help you discover the implications of the text for growing in Christ. These three keys unlock the treasures of Scripture.

Write your answers to the questions in the spaces provided or in a personal journal. Writing can bring clarity and deeper understanding of yourself and of God's Word.

5. It might be good to have a Bible dictionary handy. Use it to look up any unfamiliar words, names or places.

6. Use the prayer suggestion to guide you in thanking God for what you have learned and to pray about the applications that have come to mind.

7. You may want to go on to the suggestion under "Now or Later," or you may want to use that idea for your next study.

Suggestions for Members of a Group Study

1. Come to the study prepared. Follow the suggestions for individual study mentioned above. You will find that careful preparation will greatly enrich your time spent in group discussion.

2. Be willing to participate in the discussion. The leader of your group will not be lecturing. Instead, he or she will be encouraging the members of the group to discuss what they have learned. The leader will be asking the questions that are found in this guide.

3. Stick to the topic being discussed. Your answers should be based on the verses which are the focus of the discussion and not on outside authorities such as commentaries or speakers. These studies focus on a particular passage of Scripture. Only rarely should you refer to other portions of the Bible. This allows for everyone to participate in indepth study on equal ground.

4. Be sensitive to the other members of the group. Listen attentively when they describe what they have learned. You may be surprised by their insights! Each question assumes a variety of answers. Many questions do not have "right" answers, particularly questions that aim at meaning or application. Instead the questions push us to explore the passage more thoroughly.

When possible, link what you say to the comments of others. Also, be affirming whenever you can. This will encourage some of the more hesitant members of the group to participate.

5. Be careful not to dominate the discussion. We are sometimes so eager to express our thoughts that we leave too little opportunity for others to respond. By all means participate! But allow others to also.

6. Expect God to teach you through the passage being discussed and through the other members of the group. Pray that you will have an enjoyable and profitable time together, but also that as a result of the study you will find ways that you can take action individually and/or as a group.

7. Remember that anything said in the group is considered confidential and should not be discussed outside the group unless specific permission is given to do so.

8. If you are the group leader, you will find additional suggestions at the back of the guide.

1

Imitate Jesus

Mark 10:32-45

WWJD? We see it on bracelets, headbands, socks and hair ribbons. Why? What are people asking themselves with these four letters? For some it is a mere fashion statement—soon faded. But for many it is a minute-to-minute reminder: *What Would Jesus Do?* The phrase comes from Charles Sheldon's 1897 novel in which a small-town pastor, shaken by a dying unemployed tramp, leads his congregation to live a year based on that question. The theme of Sheldon's novel echoes, in turn, the writing of fifteenth-century monk Thomas à Kempis in *The Imitation of Christ*. Imitating Jesus has been a centuries-long goal of Christians pursuing integrity. Christ himself issued the invitation.

GROUP DISCUSSION. What would Jesus do? Describe one situation where someone you know followed that standard. What risks did that person take?

PERSONAL REFLECTION. Take time to reflect on the character of Jesus Christ. (Page through the gospels, if this helps trigger ideas.) Make a list of several qualities that are part of his character. Note also some of his actions that reflected those qualities.

Imitating Jesus was no simple matter—even when he was here in person. *Read Mark 10:32-45.*

1. This scene includes a variety of people. What differing pictures did they hold of the future?

2. Verse 32 speaks of the followers of Jesus as being both "astonished" and "afraid." What reasons did they have for feeling each of these emotions (vv. 32-34)?

3. If you had been there, how do you think you would have responded to Christ's words of verses 33-34?

4. What does the request of verse 37 suggest about the values held by James and John?

5. How do people today express similar values?

6. In what ways are you like (or not like) James and John in this setting?

7. To "drink the cup I drink" meant to share a person's fate. What did Jesus promise—and not promise (vv. 39-40)? Why?

_____

8. Study Jesus' words in verses 42-45. How does Jesus' view of greatness differ from what you normally see?

_____

9. "Not so with you," pronounces Jesus after he has described the normal leadership styles of his day. What pressures do you face to lead in the way that Christ rejects?

_____

10. Jesus creates his own definition of greatness in verses 43-45. In view of what you know of the life and works of Jesus, in what ways did he live out that description?

_____

11. How would greatness, as it is described here by Jesus, look in your church?

in your family?

in your school or workplace?

12. Pick a troubling situation in your family, church, school or workplace. To the best of your understanding, what would Jesus do in that situation?

How might you imitate him there—as you pursue the goal of integrity?

Pray to Jesus, thanking him for particular actions and character qualities that serve as a guide to you. Then bring to him specific situations where you want to imitate him, and ask for his help in doing so.

Now or Later

"Dear friends, now we are children of God, and what we will be has not yet been made known. But we know that when he appears, we shall be like him, for we shall see him as he is" (1 John 3:2). Picture your future as it is described here, and thank God for what you see.

"Everyone who has this hope in him purifies himself, just as he is pure" (1 John 3:3). What are some ways that you could begin now to become more like that future person? Ask God's help in moving that direction.

2

Keep Commitments

Commitment takes effort. We may dream of chasing the next horizon with no more hindrance than a backpack, but reality makes that vision short-term. Whether it's the implied commitment to attend classes (because your parents paid the bills) or the lifelong struggle to stay in a difficult marriage, commitment is work. A life of integrity means commitments—some of our choosing and some just the baggage of our circumstances.

GROUP DISCUSSION. What commitments are a part of your life? Each person should name one, making sure that it is different from any commitments mentioned by others in the group. On a scale of one to ten, rate yourself on how well you keep that commitment—making any explanations you wish.

PERSONAL REFLECTION. Reflect on God's commitment to you—and yours to him. Consider several specific ways that God has expressed his commitment to you. Pray, thanking him for his faithfulness. Invite God to help you examine ways you can express your commitment to him in return.

God instructed the prophet Hosea to make what seemed like an absurd commitment. *Read Hosea 1:2—2:1.*

1. If you were a counselor, what chance of success would you give this marriage? Why?

2. What connections did God make between the task he assigned to Hosea and the condition of the nation Hosea represented (1:2-4)?

3. Notice the names that God gave to each of Hosea's children. What tragedy did each name symbolize? (Look for "because" and "for" in verses 4-9.)

4. In spite of the promised losses, God also offers relief. What hope do you find here (vv. 1:7, 10-12; 2:1)?

5. What do these verses suggest about God's commitment to his people?

6. What is an experience that has made you aware of God's commitment to you?

7. Hosea 2 is a litany of the sins of Gomer and Israel, and God's promise to bring them back to himself. *Read Hosea 3.* In what ways did God ask Hosea to express his marriage commitment to Gomer?

8. In view of the information in this passage, what would make Hosea's task difficult?

_____

9. When have you made a commitment that was hard to keep?

_____

10. What is God saying about himself in these early chapters of Hosea?

_____

11. How might you begin to imitate God in one of your commitments?

Pray, thanking God for ways that he has shown his faithfulness to you.

Now or Later

Prayerfully reflect on your own commitments. Focus on a commitment that you have kept—and one that you did not. Pray about these, confessing sin if appropriate, asking help as needed. Ask God to begin to mold you into a person of integrity.

Meditate phrase by phrase on the psalm below. Talk to God about your thoughts.

> Commit your way to the LORD;
>   trust in him and he will do this:
> He will make your righteousness shine like the dawn,
>   the justice of your cause like the noonday sun. (Psalm 37:5-6)

3

Cultivate Endurance

Job 1:1—2:10

I once climbed a mountain with a bunch of high-school kids, or tried to. It sounded like such fun. And it was for awhile. They galloped ahead while I trudged behind. We saw mountain wild flowers, amazing rocks and peaks through swirling mists. I trudged higher. We stopped to take pictures and redistribute backpacks. I crawled up a field of fallen rocks, slowly. Another staffer noticed that I was pale, staggering and incoherent. It seems my physical endurance was not up to that particular task. Fortunately, the character trait of endurance is not limited to physical prowess. It shows itself in many areas: in projects, relationships and in faith.

GROUP DISCUSSION. When it comes to endurance, I am like (a) a sprinter: I commit quickly, but I finish quickly too, (b) a hurdler: I skip over the hard parts but keep running, (c) a backpacker: I hike a long distance and carry a lot of stuff, (d) an observer: I don't commit at all if I can help it, (e) a baseball player: when it rains I head to the dugout, or (f) other: _____. Explain.

PERSONAL REFLECTION. Mentally survey your history of projects, relationships and faith. In your estimation, is your endurance rating higher, lower or about right as a person of integrity. Ask God to point out what is appropriate for you in the study ahead.

Job faced an endurance test of gigantic proportions. *Read Job 1:1—2:10.*

---

1. What troubles you about this story?

---

2. What successive blows came upon Job?

---

3. How do you picture Job "before" and "after"?

---

4. What seems to be the issue of discussion between Satan and God (1:6-12; 2:1-5)?

---

5. Why was this an important subject for both Satan and God?

---

6. What additional temptations did Job's wife offer?

---

7. Notice Job's responses to pain. What do these responses suggest about Job's view of God and of himself (1:20-22; 2:10)?

8. Who won this round of the battle? Satan? God? Job? Explain.

_____

9. What benefits have come to you because of your relationship with God?

_____

10. What is your ability to endure in faith if these benefits were to be taken away?

_____

11. What project, event or relationship is currently testing your endurance? How?

_____

12. How could you better practice endurance in the ordinary events of your life?

Pray, worshiping God for who he is. Bring to mind as many names for God and as many adjectives as you can think of that describe him. Use these in your prayers of worship.

Now or Later

Can you love God for himself—not just the benefits of knowing him? Examine your own motives in God's presence, and ask God to deal with what you see.

4

Speak Truth

"The President tells lies," chortled headlines in tabloids and tribunes in 1998. In columns of fine print we later learned more than we ever wanted to know about why. It's easy to fling the whole story into the corner with disgust. But when I examine my own words and motives, I have to ask some sobering questions: What should I say to my elderly "uncle" about the *real* results of his chest x-ray? What would I say if ordered, "Recant, or die"?

GROUP DISCUSSION. Do you think a lie is ever justified? Explain.

PERSONAL REFLECTION. What situations tempt you to say what is less than true? When you consider what makes these situations tempting, what do you discover about your motives?

Abraham was on a long journey through dangerous territory. He had a convenient agreement with his wife. *Read Genesis 20.*

---

1. What is your initial reaction to each character in this story?

---

2. What does Abraham's lie in verse 2 reveal about his values?

3. Study God's words in verses 3 and 6-7. How does God show that he cares for the various people touched by Abraham's lie?

———————————————————————————————

4. What do these statements reveal about God's values?

———————————————————————————————

5. How does Abimelech show more concern for godly values than Abraham did?

———————————————————————————————

6. What do you think of Abraham's reasons for lying to Abimelech (vv. 11-13)?

———————————————————————————————

7. What circumstances do you face that make truth-telling difficult?

———————————————————————————————

8. How might a serious look at your motives help you decide how much to say—and not to say?

———————————————————————————————

9. Look at God's instructions to Abimelech in verse 7. How did Abimelech go beyond even what God asked him to do (vv. 8-16)?

10. Abimelech said to Sarah, "You are completely vindicated" (v. 16). What do you think Abraham, Abimelech and Sarah each learned from this experience?

_____

11. What harm have you seen come from failure to tell the truth?

_____

12. What forms of self-discipline would you recommend to someone who wanted to become more truthful?

Thank God for the ways that he represents truth—that his Word is truth (John 17:17). Bring to God specific areas where you fail to tell the truth. Ask his forgiveness and his help.

Now or Later

Study Psalm 15. What different areas of truth-telling does this psalm address?

What encouragement do you find here to speak truth?

The apostle Paul wrote these hopes for his friends at Ephesis: "Speaking the truth in love, we will in all things grow up into him who is the Head, that is, Christ" (Ephesians 4:15). Consider several of the areas where speaking the truth is hard for you. In view of this verse, what can you say in that setting that is both truthful and loving?

5

Practice Self-Control

"In those days there was no king in Israel; every man did what was right in his own eyes," says the closing description of the book of Judges. It was a time of national chaos and violence—Samson's era. Samson was born to devout Hebrew parents who promised to give their child to God's service. But the young adult Samson fell in love with a Philistine woman, forced both families to accept the marriage, then slaughtered thirty of his in-laws because he lost a bet. Not surprisingly, his father-in-law canceled the marriage. So Samson caught three hundred foxes, tied torches to their tails and turned them loose among the Philistines' ripened grain fields. Self-control was not Samson's specialty.

GROUP DISCUSSION. Describe a scene from your own memory where someone abandoned self-control.

PERSONAL REFLECTION. Think about a time when you failed to exercise self-control. How did this affect your relationships? Consider what this event says about how you regard yourself, others and God.

Samson judged Israel for twenty years. He was as close to a national leader as they had at that point. Then came a woman named Delilah. *Read Judges 16.*

1. What examples of Samson's failure to exercise self-control can you find in this text?

2. When you "see" the various escapades of Samson described in this chapter, what images come to your mind?

3. What does the event described in verses 1-4 reveal about the kind of person Samson was?

4. Review Delilah's four attempts to discover the source of Samson's strength and Samson's response to these attempts (vv. 4-22). What can you perceive about the relationship between these two people?

5. What character qualities in Samson made it possible for Delilah to keep her part of the bargain offered in verse 5?

6. Verses 20-21 describe the painful consequences Samson faced. When have you seen (or experienced) painful results due to lapses in self-control?

7. What do you see as the true explanation for Samson's strength—and weakness? (Compare Judges 16:20 with 14:6, 19; 15:14.)

8. Focus on verses 23-31. In what ways did the Philistines humiliate Samson?

9. Study the words of Samson's prayer in verse 28. What does it suggest about Samson's moral and spiritual condition?

10. Would you say that Samson put self-control to good or bad use in the ending of this story? Explain.

11. What are some of your strengths in the area of self-control?

What areas of self-control do you need to work on?

12. What steps can you take to move toward the kind of self-control that supports integrity? (Consider adjustments in relationships, circumstances, prayer or other appropriate steps.)

Pray, thanking God for the measure of self-control that he has already developed in you. Bring to him specific settings or circumstances that tempt you to a harmful loss of self-control. Ask for his help in those settings.

Now or Later

"The fruit of the Spirit is love, joy, peace, patience, kindness, goodness, faithfulness, gentleness and self-control" (Galatians 5:22-23). Thank God for these blessings from his Spirit as you see them in other Christians and in yourself. Spend a day doing a "fruit search." Note every time you see one of these fruit in action. At the end of your day, use your list to create a prayer of praise to God.

Consider keeping a self-control journal for a week. Note times when you have exercised appropriate self-control. Note also your lapses in this area. At the end of the week, thank God for the successes and ask that he use them for his glory. Try to notice any patterns that triggered lapses in self-control. Then prayerfully consider how you might reduce temptation or strengthen your inner resolve.

6

Respect
Your Body

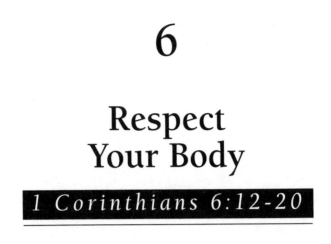

1 Corinthians 6:12-20

Four mornings a week I stumble out of bed at 5:15 and head for the gym. Even after years of this "diversion," I am still amazed at the range of bodies present there. I see pudgy young adults pumping the pedals of the bikes, elderly gentlemen stepping around the track eyeing their cardiac monitors, a grandmother who works out twice as hard as I do but weighs fifty pounds more, svelte twenty-somethings galloping through step aerobics, an obese twenty-something huffing through the same routine, three muscular guys swimming laps in triathlon training, while a gray-haired women ten feet away does water aerobics with a flotation belt to protect her arthritic knees. Anyone working out before 6:00 a.m. has got to be pretty serious about keeping fit, so I give us all an A for effort. But effort notwithstanding, our bodies wear many shapes. Even so, these shells that house our inner being are a gift from God. We are to respect our bodies and use them for his glory.

GROUP DISCUSSION. If you could change or fix one thing about your body, what would that be?

PERSONAL REFLECTION. What do you do to care for your body? How do you misuse or neglect your body? Why?

We sometimes see the Christian faith as dealing with the mind and the soul. But in this passage Paul speaks of something both solid and personal—the body. *Read 1 Corinthians 6:12-20.*

1. In what different ways throughout this text does Paul show that our bodies are important?

2. What good advice for care of the body might grow out of the statements in verses 12-13?

3. Verse 14 speaks of resurrection, Christ's and ours. Why might belief in the resurrection of the body encourage you to respect your body as it is now?

4. Verse 16 quotes the Genesis creation passage, "The two shall become one flesh." In view of the two verses on either side of this statement, what new significance does Paul bring to that ancient text?

5. What are some ways that you could allow your body to express your relationship with the Lord—that you are "one with him in spirit" (v. 17)?

6. Focus on verses 18-20. Verse 18 says that sexual sins are sins against our own bodies. What harm can come from these sins?

7. Take a moment to meditate on the statement "Do you not know that your body is a temple of the Holy Spirit" (v. 19). What feelings, questions or prayers does this bring to mind?

8. Verse 19 says, "You are not your own." How is this statement in conflict with current secular ethics?

9. What practical differences result from these two opposite views of the self? (Contrast practical expressions of current secular ethics with the way we might live out verses 18-20.)

10. In what ways do people show lack of respect for their bodies?

11. Why might a person fail to care for his or her body?

12. How can you show appropriate respect for your body—without becoming preoccupied by it?

Pray, expressing your belonging to Jesus Christ—body and soul.

Now or Later

What do you like and dislike about your body? Talk to God about some of those feelings.

Prayerfully recall your use (and misuse) of your body. If some of these actions are inconsistent with the teachings of the passage you have just studied, confess any sin against your body and ask God's help in leaving that sin. Accept the fact that he is washing away those sins— as if they had never happened.

Focus on this psalm:

> For you created my inmost being;
>   you knit me together in my mother's womb.
> I praise you because I am fearfully and wonderfully made;
>   your works are wonderful,
>   I know that full well. (Psalm 139:13-14)

Thank God for the gift of your body. If it seems appropriate, make a personal commitment to God, regarding the use of your body.

7

Expect Temptation

Genesis 39

"Lead us not into temptation," I whispered—a part of my morning prayer. Then I stopped. *What an enormous request,* I thought, *and what a strange one. Surely God would not lead me into temptation, or maybe he would—for the strengthening of my soul.* A dozen images leaped to my mind: my hidden weakness, my most vulnerable spots, my fears. "Not there," I begged God, "or there, or there," and shuddered. "Surely I could not resist that." Gradually my breathing slowed and I went on, "but deliver us from evil." ("Yes, please do," I whispered.)

Temptation comes to us: maybe not in its worst shape, but it comes. We can take comfort in Paul's promise that God "will not let you be tempted beyond what you can bear," but even that reassurance is followed with the words, "when you are tempted, . . ." (1 Corinthians 10:13). We might as well expect temptation and fortify ourselves. Prepare to resist—for it will come.

GROUP DISCUSSION. What kinds of temptations seem to be a natural part of your ordinary living?

PERSONAL REFLECTION. All of us know of situations that would tempt us to do wrong. If you were to pray "Lead us not into temptation" what specifically might you be thinking? Talk to God about this.

At one stage of his life Joseph found temptation at almost every turn. *Read Genesis 39.*

---

1. This chapter includes three scenes (vv. 1-6, 7-18, 19-23). What temptations was Joseph likely to face in each of these situations?

---

2. Focus on verses 1-6. What was good and what was difficult about Joseph's situation in Egypt?

---

3. God is mentioned several times in this section. How did he reveal himself and to whom?

---

4. Even though Joseph was a slave, he was given much power and responsibility. What temptations related to power and responsibility do you see today?

---

5. Focus on verses 7-18. What forms of sexual harassment did Joseph have to cope with from Potiphar's wife?

6. In verse 9 Joseph explained to Potiphar's wife why he refused to sleep with her. What values undergird those reasons?

---

7. What values could help people today resist the many sexual temptations of our era?

---

8. What practical steps can God's people today take to resist (or avoid) sexual temptation?

---

9. Focus on verses 19-21. Joseph did the right thing, yet he landed in jail. What does this suggest about the practical aspects of resisting temptation?

---

10. What new temptations would have faced him in prison?

---

11. God was with Joseph in prison, just as he had been with him in Potiphar's house. When have you sensed God's presence—even though everything else seemed to be going wrong?

12. Joseph seemed to expect temptation—at least enough to resist it. What temptations have you learned to expect?

13. What are some ways that you can prepare to resist temptation?

Pray aloud the Lord's Prayer. When you come to the line "lead us not into temptation but deliver us from evil," pause for a time of silent meditation and personal prayer. Then finish the prayer aloud—as your closing note of praise.

Now or Later

Make a list of current situations that tempt you to sin. (Review sins of thought, word and action.) Prayerfully consider how you might prepare yourself to resist those temptations.

Study the passage below; think your way through it phrase by phrase. Thank God for what you find there.

So, if you think you are standing firm, be careful that you don't fall! No temptation has seized you except what is common to man. And God is faithful; he will not let you be tempted beyond what you can bear. But when you are tempted, he will also provide a way out so that you can stand up under it. (1 Corinthians 10:12-13)

8

Guard
Your Tongue

James 3:1-12

"Gahp," he says with great enthusiasm. "Gahp?" he asks. I spoon mashed bananas, yogurt and a mushy greenbean mixture into his tiny rosebud mouth. "Gahp" he says again in appreciation. All things gastronomic are gahp to Thomas. I marvel at the shape of his mouth, five teeth so far, gums hiding the rest, along with buds of the next set, tongue busy all day long with giggles and yowls and the beginnings of words, a throat with vocal chords that he has somehow learned to vibrate with just the right pressure to express himself, lungs and breath forcing out the sound—at his whim. He is a marvelous creation, this grandson of mine. God made him and gave him incredible skills with a complex mechanism aimed at speech. He (and we) can use that gift for God's glory—or not.

GROUP DISCUSSION. Use your tongue to say something that you appreciate about the person sitting on your right and on your left. As long as the compliments are flowing, don't leave God out of the conversation. When you have finished talking to each other, turn to prayer. Pray one-sentence prayers of praise to God.

PERSONAL REFLECTION. Take personal inventory of how well you use your tongue. On the positive side, are you quick to encourage and to express appreciation? Are you thoughtful in what you say, so that others gain from your insight? Have you developed a listening manner? On the negative side, do you withhold words that might encourage or inform? Do you speak so often, so fast and so loudly that others do not have opportunity to express themselves? Have you perfected the art of verbal barbs so that people are injured by your words? Ask God to further reveal your verbal strengths and weaknesses as you work with the Scripture passage below.

How we use our gift of speech is important to God. *Read James 3:1-12.*

1. Notice the different objects this text uses to illustrate the tongue. How do these objects help us to picture the impact of our words?

2. Why is the use of the tongue such a good test of our character (reread v. 2)?

3. The power of speech is a gift from God, but it can also become sin. What are some sins of the tongue?

4. What inconsistencies do verses 7-12 point out?

5. How do the fig tree, grapevine and salt spring illustrate the tongue—and the source of its words?

6. Verse 8 speaks of the tongue as containing "deadly poison." When have you seen words become deadly poison?

---

7. Verse 9 says that blessing may come from the tongue. When have you been "blessed" by someone's tongue?

---

8. Verse 1 begins, "Not many of you should presume to be teachers." How might this passage help a person (who does presume to teach) to become a better teacher?

---

9. Verse 9 implies that our relationship with God ought to influence what we say to and about people. What reasons can you give for this connection?

---

10. Take a quick mental survey of your verbal strengths, skills and outright inclinations. What are some ways that you can glorify God with your tongue?

---

11. What do you consider to be your strengths and your weaknesses in the use of your tongue?

In view of these strengths and weaknesses, what steps can you take to improve the use of your tongue in one of your current relationships?

Pray, thanking God for at least one person who has spoken (or written) words of value to you. Commit to God the use of your own tongue.

Now or Later

How do you feel about the way you use words? Uncertain? Embarrassed? Frightened? Confident? Creative? Fulfilled? Other? (Perhaps these feelings vary, depending on the circumstances.) Talk to God about your feelings. Thank him for the gift of language and ask his help in using that gift in a way that honors him.

What are the pressure points that cause you to lose control of your tongue? Picture the circumstances where this is likely to occur, then bring that setting to God in prayer, making confession as needed, and asking his help in those circumstances.

Study the Scripture passages below using them as a focus for self-examination and prayer.

> The mouth of a righteous man utters wisdom,
>   and his tongue speaks what is just. (Psalm 37:30)

> Set a guard over my mouth, O LORD;
>   keep watch over the door of my lips. (Psalm 141:3)

> A gentle answer turns away wrath,
>   but a harsh word stirs up anger. (Proverbs 15:1)

9

Offer Forgiveness

John 21

"Simon, Simon, Satan has asked to sift you as wheat. But I have prayed for you, Simon, that your faith may not fail. And when you have turned back, strengthen your brothers."

But he replied, "Lord, I am ready to go with you to prison and to death."

Jesus answered, "I tell you Peter, before the rooster crows today, you will deny three times that you know me." (Luke 22:31-34)

Peter and Jesus saw the future differently. As we might expect, Peter's view of the future (and of himself) was a little shortsighted. Satan did sift Peter as wheat—and Peter flunked the test. After denying his Lord three times almost as soon as Jesus was captured, Peter disappeared from the scene. Scripture does not show him at the crucifixion. There is a brief, mysterious note in Luke 24:34 that Jesus appeared to Peter, probably on Easter Sunday morning, but we don't get to see that meeting. What we do see is an amazing account of Jesus and Peter's interaction—dealing with the problem of forgiveness.

GROUP DISCUSSION. Why is forgiveness difficult to give and to receive?

PERSONAL REFLECTION. Bring to mind a fractured relationship from your own experience. What do you need to forgive? What do need to be forgiven of?

Peter had abandoned his Lord at the time of Jesus' greatest need. Peter had seen Jesus once since then—perhaps even been forgiven—but what would their new relationship be? What role (if any) would Peter have in God's continued work? *Read John 21:1-14.*

1. Close your eyes and imagine that you are present at this event. What sights, sounds and smells surround you?

2. Try to put yourself in Peter's sandals. What are some of your thoughts and feelings?

3. In what ways did Jesus show that he wanted to continue a relationship with his disciples?

4. What would be hard about any continued relationship with Jesus at this point?

5. Jesus created an atmosphere that made it easy for his disciples to be with him. Consider one of your own difficult relationships. If you wanted to, what could you do to create a welcoming setting that might lead toward forgiveness?

---

6. *Read John 21:15-25.* What do you think was painful to Peter in his post-breakfast conversation with Jesus?

---

7. Although Jesus did not mention the word *forgiveness,* what all do you see that suggests Jesus has forgiven Peter?

---

8. What does the conversation with Jesus reveal about Peter's future responsibilities?

---

9. What do you personally find reassuring about Peter's conversation with Jesus?

---

10. What do verses 20-25 reveal about the perspective of John, the writer of this book?

11. Why is it important to learn to give and receive forgiveness?

—————————————————————————————

12. Peter was one of Jesus' closest disciples. Why is it particularly hard to forgive people who are close to you?

—————————————————————————————

13. Bring to mind one person with whom you need to extend or receive forgiveness. What is a step you could take in that direction?

Focus on the forgiveness that God has given you, the forgiving work of Jesus on your behalf. Pray, thanking God for all this brings to mind.

Now or Later

Do you suspect that you have offended someone, that perhaps you need to be forgiven? Prayerfully study Matthew 5:23-24. Then make the effort described in that passage.

Has someone hurt you to the point that you are having trouble forgiving them? Prayerfully study Matthew 18:15-22. Focus on the goal stated in verses 21-22. Then go back to the earlier part of the passage and consider what steps are appropriate for this particular relationship, steps that could lead you toward that goal.

Do you need to forgive a person no longer available to you, perhaps separated by distance or death? Notice that forgiveness does not minimize the hurt. (Jesus gave Peter the opportunity to declare his love—just as many times as he had declared his denial.) Write a letter, journal entry or prayer that could lead you to forgive that person. Then ask God's help in bringing that about.

10

Trust God

Psalm 25

I must admit that I do not do my best praying in a crisis. My mouth gets dry, my heart pounds, my body gets the shakes, my mind moves into what therapists call "catastrophizing." It's not a good scene for prayer. Somehow I'm able to move that all aside if it is someone else's crisis. But when it's *my* crisis, my prayers come out more like rabbit squeaks of "Help, God" and "Lord, have mercy." I confess that I have much growing yet needed in prayer. And in trust.

GROUP DISCUSSION. Make a timeline of your past, dividing your life by decades. As you think of the events that occurred in your life, note how that era could build your trust in God. Remember that sometimes we learn to trust out of need, sometimes out of thanksgiving. Record trust-building events on your timeline. Share your timelines and discuss: What events in your life have helped you to trust God?

PERSONAL REFLECTION. When you are in a difficult situation, what kind of prayer are you likely to pray? Ask that God will grow you in prayerful trust as you study an example of David at prayer.

David's psalms cover a huge range of emotions: anger, guilt, thanksgiving, praise—and trust. *Read Psalm 25.*

---

1. This prayer psalm divides into four stanzas (vv. 1-3, 4-7, 8-15, 16-

22). Give a topic title to each.

Which of these topics do you particularly connect with and why?

---

2. What does it mean to "lift up" your soul to God?

---

3. What do you see as the relationship between hope and trust (vv. 1-3)?

---

4. Study stanza 2 (vv. 4-7). What all does David ask God to do?

---

5. Three times David uses the term *remember.* Why would David want God to use "selective memory"?

---

6. What would you want God to remember (and forget) about you?

---

7. Study stanza 3 (vv. 6-15). In what ways does stanza 3 show that God has integrity—and therefore ought to be trusted?

8. In what ways does this stanza acknowledge David's dependence on God?

9. What do you count on God to do and to be?

10. Study stanza 4 (vv. 16-22). What words and phrases here help you to understand David's current situation?

11. Compare David's position, described in stanza 4, with what he hopes from God in verses 12-13. In view of the differences, what does David's prayer say about his own integrity?

12. How might meditating on God's character, as David did, help you to strengthen your integrity?

Pray, beginning your prayer with David's words, "To you, O LORD, I lift my soul."

Now or Later

Review the four stanzas of David's psalm. Select one idea from each stanza and write your own prayer drawing from this outline.

Leader's Notes

Leading a Bible discussion can be an enjoyable and rewarding experience. But it can also be *scary*—especially if you've never done it before. If this is your feeling, you're in good company. When God asked Moses to lead the Israelites out of Egypt, he replied, "O Lord, please send someone else to do it!" (Ex 4:13). It was the same with Solomon, Jeremiah and Timothy, but God helped these people in spite of their weaknesses, and he will help you as well.

You don't need to be an expert on the Bible or a trained teacher to lead a Bible discussion. The idea behind these inductive studies is that the leader guides group members to discover for themselves what the Bible has to say. This method of learning will allow group members to remember much more of what is said than a lecture would.

These studies are designed to be led easily. As a matter of fact, the flow of questions through the passage from observation to interpretation to application is so natural that you may feel that the studies lead themselves. This study guide is also flexible. You can use it with a variety of groups—student, professional, neighborhood or church groups. Each study takes forty-five to sixty minutes in a group setting.

There are some important facts to know about group dynamics and encouraging discussion. The suggestions listed below should enable you to effectively and enjoyably fulfill your role as leader.

Preparing for the Study

1. Ask God to help you understand and apply the passage in your own life. Unless this happens, you will not be prepared to lead others. Pray too for the various members of the group. Ask God to open your hearts

to the message of his Word and motivate you to action.

2. Read the introduction to the entire guide to get an overview of the entire book and the issues which will be explored.

3. As you begin each study, read and reread the assigned Bible passage to familiarize yourself with it.

4. This study guide is based on the New International Version of the Bible. It will help you and the group if you use this translation as the basis for your study and discussion.

5. Carefully work through each question in the study. Spend time in meditation and reflection as you consider how to respond.

6. Write your thoughts and responses in the space provided in the study guide. This will help you to express your understanding of the passage clearly.

7. It might help to have a Bible dictionary handy. Use it to look up any unfamiliar words, names or places. (For additional help on how to study a passage, see chapter five of *Leading Bible Discussions*, InterVarsity Press.)

8. Consider how you can apply the Scripture to your life. Remember that the group will follow your lead in responding to the studies. They will not go any deeper than you do.

9. Once you have finished your own study of the passage, familiarize yourself with the leader's notes for the study you are leading. These are designed to help you in several ways. First, they tell you the purpose the study guide author had in mind when writing the study. Take time to think through how the study questions work together to accomplish that purpose. Second, the notes provide you with additional background information or suggestions on group dynamics for various questions. This information can be useful when people have difficulty understanding or answering a question. Third, the leader's notes can alert you to potential problems you may encounter during the study.

10. If you wish to remind yourself of anything mentioned in the leader's notes, make a note to yourself below that question in the study.

Leading the Study

1. Begin the study on time. Open with prayer, asking God to help the group to understand and apply the passage.

2. Be sure that everyone in your group has a study guide. Encourage

the group to prepare beforehand for each discussion by reading the introduction to the guide and by working through the questions in the study.

3. At the beginning of your first time together, explain that these studies are meant to be discussions, not lectures. Encourage the members of the group to participate. However, do not put pressure on those who may be hesitant to speak during the first few sessions. You may want to suggest the following guidelines to your group.

☐ Stick to the topic being discussed.

☐ Your responses should be based on the verses which are the focus of the discussion and not on outside authorities such as commentaries or speakers.

☐ These studies focus on a particular passage of Scripture. Only rarely should you refer to other portions of the Bible. This allows for everyone to participate in in-depth study on equal ground.

☐ Anything said in the group is considered confidential and will not be discussed outside the group unless specific permission is given to do so.

☐ We will listen attentively to each other and provide time for each person present to talk.

☐ We will pray for each other.

4. Have a group member read the introduction at the beginning of the discussion.

5. Every session begins with a group discussion question. The question or activity is meant to be used before the passage is read. The question introduces the theme of the study and encourages group members to begin to open up. Encourage as many members as possible to participate and be ready to get the discussion going with your own response.

This section is designed to reveal where our thoughts or feelings need to be transformed by Scripture. That is why it is especially important not to read the passage before the discussion question is asked. The passage will tend to color the honest reactions people would otherwise give because they are, of course, supposed to think the way the Bible does.

You may want to supplement the group discussion question with an icebreaker to help people to get comfortable. See the community section of *Small Group Idea Book* for more ideas.

You also might want to use the personal reflection question with your group. Either allow a time of silence for people to respond individually or discuss it together.

6. Have a group member (or members if the passage is long) read aloud the passage to be studied. Then give people several minutes to read the passage again silently so that they can take it all in.

7. Question 1 will generally be an overview question designed to briefly survey the passage. Encourage the group to briefly survey the passage, but try to avoid getting sidetracked by questions or issues that will be addressed later in the study.

8. As you ask the questions, keep in mind that they are designed to be used just as they are written. You may simply read them aloud. Or you may prefer to express them in your own words.

There may be times when it is appropriate to deviate from the study guide. For example, a question may have already been answered. If so, move on to the next question. Or someone may raise an important question not covered in the guide. Take time to discuss it, but try to keep the group from going off on tangents.

9. Avoid answering your own questions. If necessary, repeat or rephrase them until they are clearly understood. Or point out something you read in the leader's notes to clarify the context or meaning. An eager group quickly becomes passive and silent if they think the leader will do most of the talking.

10. Don't be afraid of silence. People may need time to think about the question before formulating their answers.

11. Don't be content with just one answer. Ask, "What do the rest of you think?" or "Anything else?" until several people have given answers to the question.

12. Acknowledge all contributions. Try to be affirming whenever possible. Never reject an answer. If it is clearly off-base, ask, "Which verse led you to that conclusion?" or again, "What do the rest of you think?"

13. Don't expect every answer to be addressed to you, even though this will probably happen at first. As group members become more at ease, they will begin to truly interact with each other. This is one sign of healthy discussion.

14. Don't be afraid of controversy. It can be very stimulating. If you don't resolve an issue completely, don't be frustrated. Move on and keep it in mind for later. A subsequent study may solve the problem.

15. Periodically summarize what the group has said about the passage. This helps to draw together the various ideas mentioned and gives continuity to the study. But don't preach.

16. At the end of the Bible discussion you may want to allow group members a time of quiet to work on an idea under "Now or Later." Then discuss what you experienced. Or you may want to encourage group members to work on these ideas between meetings. Give an opportunity during the session to allow people to talk about what they are learning.

17. Conclude your time together with conversational prayer, adapting the prayer suggestion at the end of the study to your group. Ask for God's help in following through on the commitments you've made.

18. End on time.

Many more suggestions and helps are found in *Leading Bible Discussions*, which is part of the LifeGuide Bible Study series.

Components of Small Groups

A healthy small group should do more than study the Bible. There are four components to consider as you structure your time together.

Nurture. Small groups help us to grow in our knowledge and love of God. Bible study is the key to making this happen and is the foundation of your small group.

Community. Small groups are a great place to develop deep friendships with other Christians. Allow time for informal interaction before and after each study. Plan activities and games that will help you to get to know each other. Spend time having fun together—going on a picnic or cooking dinner together.

Worship and prayer. Your study will be enhanced by spending time praising God together in prayer or song. Pray for each other's needs—and keep track of how God is answering prayer in your group. Ask God to help you to apply what you are learning in your study.

Outreach. Reaching out to others can be a practical way of applying what you are learning, and it will keep your group from becoming self-focused. Host a series of evangelistic discussions for your friends or neighbors. Clean up the yard of an elderly friend. Serve at a soup kitchen together, or spend a day working on a Habitat house.

Many more suggestions and helps in each of these areas are found in

Small Group Idea Book. Information on building a small group can be found in *Small Group Leaders' Handbook* and *The Big Book on Small Groups* (both from InterVarsity Press). Reading through one of these books would be worth your time.

Study 1. Imitate Jesus. Mark 10:32-45.

Purpose: To imitate the character and actions of Jesus in current troubling situations.

Group discussion. Try to involve each person present with this question. Draw on personal experience, acquaintances or even reports in the media. The object is to help the group discover that imitating Jesus is possible and involves specific actions, but it may include risk.

Personal reflection. These questions are designed for individuals studying on their own. However, they also work well in a group if people are allowed a few minutes of silence to reflect on them as they prepare for study.

Question 1. Use this question to gain an overview of the passage. Try to find the view of the future for the ten disciples, Jesus, James and John, and the crowd. While the view of the crowd is not specific (they "were afraid," v. 32), there is a stark contrast between what Jesus saw ahead and what James and John hoped for. This is Jesus' last trip to Jerusalem; he knows that he is headed for the cross.

Question 4. The request of these disciples implies that they wanted to be near the source of power; they wanted to look good, be above others, have control or any number of other motives. Many of these are motives close to our own hearts.

Augustine, who lived from A.D. 354 to 430, observed:

> Ponder how profound this is. They were conferring with him about glory. He intended to precede loftiness with humility and, only through humility, to read the way for loftiness itself. For, of course, even those disciples who wanted to sit, the one on his right, the other on his left, were looking to glory. They were on the lookout, but did not see by what way. In order that they might come to their homeland in due order, the Lord called them back to the narrow way. For the homeland is on high and the way to it is lowly. The homeland is life in Christ; the way is dying with Christ. The way is suffering with Christ; the goal is abiding with him eternally. Why do you seek

the homeland if you are not seeking the way to it? (quoted in *Mark*, Ancient Christian Commentary on Scripture, Thomas C. Oden and Christopher A. Hall, eds. [Downers Grove, Ill.: InterVarsity Press, 1998], p. 149.)

Question 6. It would be easy to fault James and John if they were not so much like ourselves. We too might want to be near power, to get our bid in before others. We too are sometimes not "tuned in" to important conversations in our presence. Or maybe we just like to plan ahead. Not all of these similarities are bad—depending on how we use them. It is some encouragement to know that in spite of their jarring performance in this scene, both James and John became faithful leaders in the early church.

Question 7. If you want an extra question after this one, ask: Why do you think the other ten disciples were angry at James and John? (They may have wanted the same position. Or they may have been angry at the inappropriateness of the request.)

Question 9. Most of us face a variety of internal and external pressures to lead in this ordinary way. We may have an internal desire to control, to be in charge, to make things work efficiently. Or we may have external pressures to get the numbers right on a job (or in the church or student group). Or we may want to get into a position of power so that, once there, we can "do good."

Question 11. Try to be as specific as possible as you consider this question. For example, how might Jesus' kind of greatness look in a Sunday-school teacher working with third graders? When the church board deals with a controversial issue? When the pastor walks to the pulpit?

In your family, how might his greatness look when a teenager asks to borrow the family car—and in how the parent responds?

In your school, how might it look in a dispute about schedules or grades? How might your philosophy class look if the college president/professor/student practiced this kind of greatness? Be as specific (and as relevant to your own situation) as you can.

Chrysostom, who lived from about 350 to 407 wrote in *On the Incomprehensible Nature of God*, "God wants for nothing and has need of nothing. Yet, when he humbled himself, he produced such great good, increased his household, and extended his kingdom. Why, then, are you afraid that you will become less if you humble yourself?"

Question 12. It's sometimes difficult to translate the first century actions of Jesus into current settings when we ask the question "What would Jesus do?" If the circumstances are vastly different, we can focus on the character of Jesus—and move from there to actions we think are likely in our current setting. Use these principles as you focus on your own current situations.

Study 2. Keep Commitments. Hosea 1:1—2:1; 3.

Purpose: To model God's example of commitment to his people by honoring our own commitments.

Group discussion. Since many of us have similar commitments, the challenge here will be to name a commitment not yet named by someone else in the group. Samples include: marriage vows, projects, appointments, volunteer tasks, friendships, practice of faith, contracts, bill-paying, due dates, promises to children (or parents), getting to work on time, attending classes and so on. The rating system and explanations can be rather lighthearted. The object here is not to conduct an intense confessional but to begin thinking together of the wide array of commitments normal to life—and the way we handle these.

Question 1. Was Gomer a prostitute at the time Hosea married her? Or is the statement of verse 2 simply a warning that she would become a prostitute? The answer is uncertain, but the *New Bible Commentary* suggests that God would probably not have instructed Hosea to break his own law given in Leviticus 21:15-15 and Deuteronomy 22:13-21. Instead, this statement may have meant that Gomer came from an environment where prostitution is considered normal, or (more likely) that she would become a prostitute during the course of their marriage.

Question 3. Did these children biologically belong to Hosea? The text is uncertain, though Jezreel seems to be his. Verse 3 says, "Gomer . . . bore him a son." As for the next two children, the text of chapter 1 and especially chapter 2 make it seem likely that they were not.

If you can use an additional question at this point, ask, Even though it seems cruel to name a child with these terms, what reminders would these names give to anyone who used them?

Question 4. The nation of Israel would eventually be overrun by the Assyrians and (in the eyes of history) become completely annihilated.

How then could the promise of God in verses 9-10 come to pass? Several explanations are possible: First, many of the people of Israel fled south and mingled with their sister nation of Judah thus creating a blended people. Second, in a spiritual sense Jesus Christ came as Messiah, their "one leader." Third, the Christian church unites God's people into a single body. These explanations may not satisfy all objections but can point us in a reasonable direction.

Question 6. Pause long enough at this point to reflect on several experiences with God that show the extent of his commitment. If you are in a group, be prepared to tell of a brief experience of your own that will invite others to respond similarly.

If you have time for a longer study, you may want to read Hosea 2:2-23 and ask the following questions: According to verses 2-13, what all has Gomer (and the nation of Israel) done wrong? Verse 14 begins with the word *therefore*. In what ways will God respond to his people (vv. 14-23)? (Notice in verses 22-23 that the threats implied by the names of each of the three children are now turned into related blessings.)

Question 9. For a possible follow-up ask, When have you been glad that someone kept a commitment to you?

Question 10. God reveals much of his character in these early chapters of Hosea. Aspects to consider are his holiness, wrath, tenacity, commitment to his people, mercy, faithfulness. Consider why God wants to make an example of Hosea and Gomer.

Study 3. Cultivate Endurance. Job 1:1—2:10.

Purpose: To cultivate endurance in the large and small issues of our lives.

Group discussion. Encourage each person to participate to the extent possible. Be sure to focus on endurance as a character trait, not as mere physical ability.

Question 1. Many potential problems show up with an initial reading of this story. Why were God and Satan talking with each other? Why did God allow Satan to torment Job? Why were the animals, servants and children destroyed in a battle that had nothing to do with them? Why did Job accept his troubles? Why didn't God let Job know what was going on? What was the real battle about? Did Job suffer because he was good? Most of us would find these questions troubling, especially if something similar happened to us.

Question 2. Notice the five stages of Job's disaster in 1:13-15, 16, 17, 18-19; 2:7-8.

Question 3. Create mental pictures from the information you find in 1:1-5, 20-22; 2:7-10.

Question 4. Study 1:6-12 and 2:1-5. It is interesting to notice that each time it is God who initiates the discussion about Job. Why? What is God trying to prove with this trial? According to the *New Bible Commentary*, "Sometimes, as in the case of Job himself, suffering comes for no earthly reason at all but simply in order to justify God's claim that humans can serve him without thought of reward" ([Downers Grove, Ill.: InterVarsity Press, 1994], p. 459). This is the complaint that Satan makes in his accusation of 1:9-11. It is as if Satan is taunting God, suggesting that people love him only for what they can get for themselves. If those benefits were taken away, human commitment to God would cease. (It would be a risky test for most of us.)

Note: Regarding Satan's taunt "Skin for skin" of 2:4, this was probably a proverb of the day suggesting that people care most for their own "skin." Job has saved his skin by not rejecting God after the deaths of his children. But if it is *his* skin (body) under attack, he will crumple. It is interesting to note that the next attack comes literally on Job's skin.

Question 5. It is possible to do the right things for the wrong reasons—and Satan, in his crafty insights, attacks motives. He suggests that Job's acts of righteousness have nothing to do with worship of God. Instead, his righteous acts are simply a con game; he plays by the rules in order to get what he wants from a superior Being. *The NIV Study Bible* comments:

> When God calls up the name of Job before the accuser and testifies to the righteousness of this one on the earth—this man in whom God delights— Satan attempts with one crafty thrust both to assail God's beloved and to show up God as a fool. True to one of his modes of operation, he accuses Job before God. He charges that Job's godliness is evil. The very godliness in which God takes delight is void of all integrity; it is the worst of all sins. Job's godliness is self-serving; he is righteous only because it pays. If God will only let Satan tempt Job by breaking the link between righteousness and blessing, he will expose the righteous man for the sinner he is.
>
> It is the adversary's ultimate challenge. For if the godliness of the righ-

teous man in whom God delights can be shown to be the worst of all sins, then a chasm of alienation stands between them that cannot be bridged. Then even redemption is unthinkable, for the godliest of men will be shown to be the most ungodly. God's whole enterprise in creation and redemption will be shown to be radically flawed, and God can only sweep it all away with awful judgment.

The accusation, once raised, cannot be removed, not even by destroying the accuser. So God lets the adversary have his way with Job (within specified limits) so that God and the righteous Job may be vindicated and the great accuser silenced. Thus comes the anguish of Job, robbed of every sign of God's favor so that God becomes for him the great enigma. ([Grand Rapids, Mich.: Zondervan, 1994], p. 732)

Question 7. Study the information in 2:9-10. A host of temptations flow out of her brief words: Job should kill himself—or invite God to kill him. His integrity was worth nothing. He should curse God. Death was better than the life God had given him. In kindness to Job's wife, we should note that her grief must have equaled or exceeded Job's. And it appears that she was not even committed to this God of his. Or perhaps the multiple tragedies had temporarily destroyed her faith. In any event, Job's answer fits his character: his words are wise and speak of endurance.

Question 9. Who was on trial? It appears that God was on trial—and that God chose Job to illustrate his defense. Satan's accusation was that people serve God only because he pays them back. Job's response proves that this is not necessarily true. *Some* serve God even without visible benefits. Job, for example.

Question 10. Consider physical, emotional, relational and spiritual benefits.

Question 13. None of us wants a Job-type of experience. But suffering of some sort will come to us without invitation. We can strengthen the quality of endurance in our character by practicing on the small events of our lives that require this trait. That may mean maintaining a difficult and unrewarding friendship, staying in an important class even though dropping it would be easier and more convenient, working to improve a troubled church rather than moving on to the happy church down the road, or burning the "midnight oil" on a long overdue project. Endurance counts—if the goal is building integrity.

Study 4. Speak Truth. Genesis 20.

Purpose: To consider the difficulties in telling the truth and to learn to lovingly speak the truth anyway.

Group discussion. Your group should have a variety of opinions on this subject. Most will think that under certain circumstances a lie might be the least harmful of a variety of choices. It's the explanation of *why* it might be all right to lie that ought to stir interest. This will prepare you to identify with Abraham's dilemma. Abraham thought he had a good reason to lie, under the circumstances.

Question 1. Take a good look at each of the three main characters of this event: Abraham, Sarah and Abimelech. Consider not only what they did but why they did it.

Question 2. Notice Abraham's relative concern for Sarah, Abimelech, Abimelech's people and himself. His action appears to put more value on himself than on anyone else, a frequent source of lying. A follow-up question might be, Do you think that Abraham loved his wife?

Did Abraham's marriage to Sarah break God's laws? God had not yet given a law to his people regarding marriage to close family members. Leviticus 20:17 says, "If a man marries his sister, the daughter of either his father or his mother, and they have sexual relations, it is disgrace. They must be cut off before the eyes of their people." But that law came to Moses some 600 years after the time of Abraham.

Question 6. Was Sarah really Abraham's half-sister? Information about Abraham's family appears in Genesis 11:27-32. But Sarah is mentioned only as his wife. Scripture does not elsewhere define her parentage. Even so, Abraham illustrates a universal problem for those who lie. Because of one lie, his words on similar subjects face disbelief. We feel, justifiably, that we must prove his words from some outside source. Four thousand years later, readers cannot *know* that Sarah was Abraham's half-sister just because he said it.

Adding to the seriousness of Abraham's deceit is the promise that God gave to him and Sarah just two chapters back. God promised that Abraham and Sarah would have a son (Gen 18:10). Within weeks, it seems, Abraham was willing to jeopardize the paternity of that son—in order to save his own skin.

Question 9. We may wonder why God allowed Abraham to profit from his lie. Meredith G. Kline, writing in the *New Bible Commentary,* says, "By his lavish gifts Abimelech would have Sarah forget her experience in his court. . . . In spite of indignity suffered, Sarah's honour was by the royal gift restored in the eyes of others" (p. 98).

Along similar lines Gleason L. Archer, writing in *Encyclopedia of Bible Difficulties,* says: "Abraham showed a lack of confidence in God's power to preserve him from mortal danger and failed to uphold God's honor before the eyes of the unbelieving world. Even though he was given a thousand shekels by way of atonement for Abimelech's having taken Sarah into his palace, Abraham had to leave under a cloud of dishonor. . . . This account no more exonerates Abraham from his sin than did the similar adventure in Egypt. He came away from both failures with dishonor and shame, and his influence on the Philistines was as nullified as it had been in the case of the Egyptians" (p. 90).

Question 11. This is a good point to think of stories, actual events where you have seen harm come from a lie. That harm might come to the person who told the lie, to those who heard it or both.

Question 12. Consider ways to practice truth-telling, especially truth spoken in love. Consider also ways to minimize damage once a lie has been told. It's possible that we must deal not only with the actual practice of what we say but also the motives behind what we say. Why do we want someone else to hear what is less than true? How can we change those motives?

Study 5. Practice Self-Control. Judges 16.

Purpose: To observe from Samson's life the danger of lapses in self-control, and to learn to use appropriate self-control in our own circumstances.

Group discussion. Involve as many people as possible in response to this question. Abandoning self-control might be joyful or tragic. There is no need to recount only the most horrific experiences. Even small lapses will help set the atmosphere for entering the life of Samson.

Personal reflection. Some lapses in self-control are good, especially for those of us who are more up-tight or self-contained than is emotionally healthy. A good healthy scream on the downhill plunge of a roller coaster cleans out the emotional pipes. But many lapses in self-control are, at heart, selfish acts. These lapses see personal expression as of greater worth than the damage that expression many inflict on someone else. Lack of self-control says, "I am more important than you are." Refusal to exercise self-control can also underestimate God. It says, "God is kind; he understands; he will forgive me." But it does not properly apprehend God's holiness or his judgment. And refusal to exercise self-control is self-indulgent. It is a lazy approach to life that says, "I am what I am. Why change?"

Question 5. What did it mean to be a Nazirite? J. B. Payne, writing in *The Zondervan Pictorial Encyclopedia of the Bible,* explains that a Nazirite was a member of a Hebrew religious class especially dedicated to God. God gave instructions for this order in Numbers 6:1-12, just before the Hebrews left Mt. Sinai. Nazirites took voluntary vows, either in person or on the strength of their parents' vows. They were not to touch any dead body. They were not to use any grape products. And they were not to shave or cut their hair. Some people took these vows for a limited period of time. The apostle Paul did so in Acts 18:18. Others, like Samuel, John the Baptist and Samson, took vows that extended for a lifetime. Nazirites were to make themselves always available for use by God. He or she was to lead the people of Israel in devotion to God (vol. 4, pp. 392-93).

The *New Bible Commentary* suggests the startling idea that Samson may have been hoping that his relationship with Delilah would get him out of the Nazirite vow taken by his parents. Perhaps he saw her as his last chance to have a normal life, to become an ordinary man. But it was not just his Nazirite position that he was giving up; he was also forming an alliance with a Philistine woman—at terrible expense.

Be sure to note the "deal" offered Delilah in verse 5. According to *The NIV Study Bible* the money may have been equivalent to the cost of 275 slaves (p. 350). (See also Genesis 37:28 for the price paid for Joseph several centuries earlier.)

Question 7. What was the secret of Samson's strength? Samson seemed to think that it was in his hair, but was it? In their *Commentary on the Old Testament,* Keil and Delitzsch say no. "The superhuman strength of Samson did not reside in his hair as hair, but in the fact the Jehovah was with or near him. But Jehovah was with him so long as he maintained his condition as a Nazirite. As soon as he broke away from this by sacrificing the hair which he wore in honour of the LORD, Jehovah departed from him, and with Jehovah went his strength" (*Joshua, Judges, Ruth, 1 & 2 Samuel*, p. 423).

Question 9. As in most of our own prayers, we find in Samson's prayer what is good and also what is less than honorable. A phrase by phrase study of his words reveals much to admire including his admission that God is "sovereign" and his desire for a continued relationship with God. The word *revenge,* however stands out as less than admirable. Barry G. Webb writing in the *New Bible Commentary* reflects, "Earlier he had asked for life (15:18-19); now he asked for death. Even in death his motives were not pure; he sought personal revenge rather than the glory of God. But at least he did at last do what he had been finally set apart to do, and the victory was unquestionably the Lord's."

Question 10. There is no obvious answer to this question; we might reasonably defend either side. A follow-up question might be: Was Samson's death a suicide or a sacrifice? We can also reflect on certain vague similarities to Christ's death.

Question 11. After studying Samson as an example, we might well think of self-control as control over anger and violence. This would let us mild-mannered Christians off the hook far too easily. Our own temptation to lapses in self-control might include wasting time, overeating, sexual temptations, angry words, gossip and a host of other *sins* that require the discipline of self-control. Use these questions to examine your own strengths and also your vulnerable areas.

Study 6. Respect Your Body. 1 Corinthians 6:12-20.

Purpose: To value our bodies as a gift from God and as a temple of the Holy Spirit.

Group discussion. Create lighthearted interaction here. The purpose is to acknowledge that our bodies are less than perfect, that we are powerless to fix much of what is wrong but that they are important to us anyway.

Personal reflection. Most of us pamper our body in some ways and neglect it in others. Too much pampering can get self-centered. Too much neglect is harmful and disrespectful to this gift from God. It will help you gain perspective and balance if you can take a good look at your motives for each.

Question 1. Survey the passage with this questions. Answers appear in nearly every verse.

Question 2. These two verses raise a variety of principles: the difference between what is permissible and what is beneficial, the impermanence of both food and stomach, the impact of sexual immorality. Think of several bits of advice that might grow out of these principles. For example, just because you *can* doesn't mean you *should*. Even if you eat a whole tray of brownies today, you'll be hungry again tomorrow. Sexual immorality is *not* natural. Make your advice as specific to your own setting as seems important.

"Food for the stomach and the stomach for food" was probably a common saying of the era. Paul uses that saying to point out the flaws in thinking that what we do with our bodies doesn't have much importance. *NIV Study Bible* comments:

> Paul quotes some Corinthians again who were claiming that as the physical acts of eating and ingesting food have no bearing on one's inner spiritual life, so the physical act of promiscuous sexual activity does not affect one's spiritual life. The body is not meant for sexual immorality, but for the Lord. Paul here declares the dignity of the human body: It is intended for the Lord. Although granting that food and the stomach are transitory, Paul denies that what one does with his body is unimportant. This is particularly true of the use of sex, which the Lord has ordained in wedlock. (p. 1743)

Question 4. Verse 15 contains a warning about sexual immorality. It seems to imply that the physical union with a prostitute creates connections far beyond the moment. On the other hand, verse 17 speaks of being united with Jesus Christ. Even though this is a union of the spirit, our physical connections can impact our ability to be close to Jesus.

Question 8. Current secular ethics teach that we belong to ourselves alone. We must take charge of our own lives. We must not allow others to manipulate us. We must first look at "What's in it for me?" If we don't take care of ourselves, no one else will. As for sex, this is often considered a recreational activity of little consequence beyond the moment. Christian ethics, as expressed in this chapter and elsewhere, say that this is not true at all. We are not our own. We belong body and soul to Jesus Christ

(vv. 19-10). Our bodies and their sexual gifts belong to our spouses, as Paul explains further into his argument (1 Cor 7:4-5). We are to love and care for each other, sharing our needs and our talents (1 Cor 12). We are to love our neighbor as much as we love ourselves (Mt 19:19).

Study 7. Expect Temptation. Genesis 39.

Purpose: To recognize temptations particular to our own circumstances—and to prepare to resist them.

Group discussion. Encourage several to participate in this question. Even though we all live in the same world, each of us has our own particular pressures to do wrong. Other temptations are common to all of us. This area of discussion will come up in more depth later in the study.

Question 1. Even without knowing how Joseph responded in each setting, it is possible to guess what temptations are likely to appear in each circumstance: caretaker of a rich man's household, propositioned by the boss's wife, unjustly imprisoned and in charge of the other prisoners. Temptations include attitudes as well as actions. They also include issues of faith in God—and unbelief.

Question 4. Use this question to move from Joseph's era to our own. Consider temptations that occur in the context of power and responsibility, in the general course of events. But don't be afraid to look at your own temptations in a similar context. You do not have to be a CEO to misuse power and responsibility. These same temptations follow us to our homes, friendships and churches.

Question 6. Study Joseph's values as they relate to his work, his employer (slave owner) and his God.

Questions 7-8. These questions are related but separate. In question 7 examine first the *values* that could help people resist sexual temptation. These might include our values about family, faith, God, the future, even our own bodies. But values will only take us so far. Beyond that, we must also take practical steps, which question 8 implies. It will take many practical steps to put those values into action if we are to resist the temptations of our sex-saturated era. Try to be as specific as possible in responding to each of these questions.

Question 10. This section of the text does not speak of specific temptations, but if we put ourselves in Joseph's shoes we should have no trouble imagining the temptations he faced. He has been jailed unjustly; he has charge of fellow prisoners—and the warden is paying no attention. Apart from the obvious practical temptations, he might also be facing temptations toward bitterness and toward unbelief in God.

Question 11. Derek Kidner writing in the Tyndale Old Testament Commentary series says, "The symmetry of this chapter, in which the serene opening (1-6) is matched, point for point, at a new level at the close (19-23) despite all that intervenes, perfectly expresses God's quiet control and the man of faith's quiet victory. The good seed is buried deeper, still to push upward; the servant, faithful in a little, trains for authority in much" (*Genesis* [Downers Grove, Ill.: InterVarsity Press, 1967], p. 189).

The example of God's continued presence with Joseph sets a backdrop with which to reflect on God's mercies to us, even during our own dark times.

Study 8. Guard Your Tongue. James 3:1-12.

Purpose: To use God's gift of speech for his glory.

Personal reflection. This is not an occasion to conjure up inappropriate guilt. On the contrary, mentally survey the gift of speech that God has given to you—and how you use it. If there are weaknesses, perhaps the study ahead will help you find ways to correct them. If there are strengths, pray that God will help you find ways to use them to glorify him.

Question 1. Objects representing the tongue appear in almost every verse of this passage. You should find at least seven objects, then consider briefly their meaning.

Question 3. Sins of the tongue are often considered "soft sins," sins that we don't think much about. Yet the objects illustrating sins of the tongue in this passage hint at nothing soft. Typical sins include gossip, angry words, slander, cursing, lying, self-aggrandizement, verbal put-downs and others.

Question 5. Peter H. Davids, writing in the *New Bible Commentary*, says of verse 9:

We use our tongues to praise God. But then we speak evil of (curse in his words—any speaking against a person can be in effect a curse) other people, and they are made in God's image (Gn. 1:26-27; 9:6). In James's day the king or emperor would set up his statue in the cities of his realm. If anyone insulted or cursed the statue, they were treated as if they had cursed the emperor to his face, for the statue was the image of the emperor. Therefore the insulting of a person, made in God's image, is like insulting God himself. This duality, two different and contradictory words coming out of the same mouth is a type of hypocrisy. (p. 1363)

Verses 11 and 12 give further examples of inconsistencies and encourage us to look not only at the problem but the source.

Question 6. Just as water and fruit testify of their source, so do our words. What comes out of our mouths speaks of what is inside us. If we are speaking in anger or hatred or deceit, we would do well to look at our motives—even if we are praising God out of the other corner of our mouth.

Question 9. If you need a clarifying question, ask: How does your own relationship with God impact your words to and about people? or, How would you like your relationship between God to impact your relationship with certain people?

Question 10. We can glorify God in obvious ways: singing, praying, preaching, teaching and sharing our faith. Try to also consider more subtle ways that you can express God's glory to him—and to people.

Study 9. Offer Forgiveness. John 21.

Purpose: To follow the example of Jesus and Peter by giving and receiving forgiveness.

Group discussion. Forgiveness for small slights is simple: "Pardon me for bumping you." "Sure, no problem." But the hard work of forgiveness comes when the hurt is deep and prolonged—and sometimes not even acknowledged. Furthermore, like gifts, forgiveness is sometimes easier to give than to receive. Encourage the group to begin thinking about these difficulties as they approach the subject of forgiveness.

Personal reflection. Begin now to think of relationships that need the work of forgiveness. Plan to do more detailed work near the end of the study and in the "Now or Later" section.

Question 2. Peter is quite active in this scene; his thoughts and feelings probably changed from one episode to the next. Consider how he felt during the night of fishing when he heard the announcement from John, during his splashing walk through the sea, at breakfast.

Question 3. Spot pieces of information throughout the text.

Question 4. The disciples must have been incredibly confused about who Jesus was and any future role he might have in their lives. It appears that none of the disciples had stood by him during his death—except John—and now Jesus is alive again. (Were they embarrassed about their cowardice?) They must have wondered what kind of relationship they could have with Jesus. Yet, for some reason he is cooking them breakfast. But wasn't he going to disappear again soon? Besides, they knew they had been mistaken about hopes of a political kingdom headed by Jesus. What else had then been mistaken about?

Question 6. The biblical text provides several clues to Peter's dilemma. What would it be like to be asked three times about his love for Jesus? Was he reminded of his threefold denial? Did he see it as an opportunity to recommit to Jesus in equal amount? Was he grateful for the new three-fold challenge that Jesus offered—or frightened of the responsibility— now that he knows all too well his weaknesses? Even as he affirms his love for Jesus, can he trust himself to keep that love?

Question 8. Notice the slightly different instructions of verses 16-17 as well as the prediction of verse 18—and what these convey about responsibilities.

Question 9. Focus on the character of Jesus as it is revealed in this post-resurrection encounter beside the sea. If we are wise, we approach Jesus with a sense of our own wrongdoing. Yet, if Jesus welcomed Peter, even trusted him with kingdom work, he might do the same for us.

Question 11. Forgiveness is hard, but it is also important. We have the commands of Christ—given at an earlier time to Peter himself (Mt 18:22-23). We also have Jesus as an example in this story. Besides, since we can come to God only as sinners needing forgiveness, how could we refuse to extend that grace to other people? Then there are the personal relationships established by the image of the church, symbolized by a single body—Christ's body (1 Cor 12:12-31). How can we coexist in a single body without constant forgiveness? Beyond that, we must also be conscious of our image to those outside the faith, as we invite them to share the grace of belonging to God's family. Jesus said, "By this all men will know that you are my disciples, if you love one another" (Jn 13:35).

Study 10. Trust God. Psalm 25.

Purpose: To trust God as we draw on the integrity of God as a model for our own.

Group discussion. You will need to allow 20 minutes or more for this activity, but you will find it worthwhile for what you learn about yourself and one another. If you are short on time, sharing in pairs will keep things moving.

Question 2. Don't look for a single "correct answer." Capture some of the ideals of worship as individuals express how they lift their souls to God.

Question 4. Study the verbs in verses 4-7.

Question 6. Conduct a personal, thoughtful discussion of this question. Then, if time permits a follow-up question, ask, What are you saying about God (and yourself) when you ask that he not remember certain things?

Question 7. Almost every phrase in verse 8-15 will contribute an answer to this question.

Question 8. Move the focus from God to David with this question.

Question 10. Likely words include *lonely, afflicted, troubles, anguish, affliction, distress* and *enemies.* Note also David's need for "rescue" and "refuge."

Question 11. We do not know the details of David's circumstances, but his descriptive words suggest a Job-like condition. Yet, verses 12-13 reflect an entirely different expectation. Even though these expectations are not yet met (and may not ever come to pass), David continues to worship God and commit himself to God. Though he speaks of God's integrity, his prayer of worship and commitment also reflect his own.

Question 12. If you need a more pointed follow-up question, ask, What specific aspects of God's character would you like to imitate in order to have more integrity?

Of verse 21 *NIV Study Bible* says, "*Integrity and uprightness.* Personified virtues. . . . Pardon is not enough; David prays that God will enable him to live a life of unmarred moral rectitude—even as God is 'good and upright' (v. 8)" (p. 803).

Carolyn Nystrom is a freelance writer and editor. She and her husband Roger live in St. Charles, Illinois. Carolyn is also the author of the LifeGuide® Bible Studies 1 & 2 Peter and Jude, Old Testament Kings, New Testament Characters and Friendship, as well as the Women of Character guide A Woman of Family.